Colors in My World

Purple in My World

By Brienna Rossiter

level
1
little blue
readers

www.littlebluehousebooks.com

Little Blue House is distributed by North Star Editions:
sales@northstareditions.com | 888-417-0195

Produced for Little Blue House by Red Line Editorial.

Photographs ©: Shutterstock Images, cover, 4, 7, 8–9, 12–13, 15, 16 (top left), 16 (bottom right); iStockphoto, 11, 16 (top right), 16 (bottom left)

Library of Congress Control Number: 2020900833

ISBN
978-1-64619-160-4 (hardcover)
978-1-64619-194-9 (paperback)
978-1-64619-262-5 (ebook pdf)
978-1-64619-228-1 (hosted ebook)

Printed in the United States of America
Mankato, MN
082020

About the Author

Brienna Rossiter enjoys playing music, reading books, and drinking tea. She lives in Minnesota.

Table of Contents

I See Purple

I see flowers.

The flowers are purple.

I see kites.

The kites are purple.

I wear boots.

The boots are purple.

boot

I ride a bike.

The bike is purple.

I build with blocks.

The blocks are purple.

I do a craft.

The paint is purple.

paint

Glossary

bike

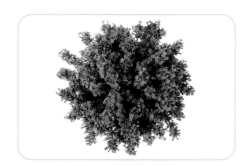

flowers

craft

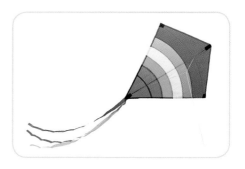

kite

Index